Index

Introduction

With the economy falling, people losing their jobs left and right, the inflation of prices, and the costs of living rising everyday… What can be done?

Realize there are simply things out of our control and we cannot run from them. When we have a daunting obstacle in front of us, we can cower in fear, try to run, or face it head on. One of those huge obstacles is employment. People put their faith and the fate of their families in the hands of corporations or the economy. Some people who have worked in one place as long as 40+ years are now being laid-off without benefits, retirement or 401k. It's sad to say more people have lost not only their job but their homes and families. It is an economical struggle we are all starting to feel.

So what can help you pay the bills, keep your house, pay off your debts, if you are not employed?

The answer is; **provide a service.** When employed at a job, you are providing a service to the customer or to your employer, and that is how you make money. The greater the service you provide, the greater pay you'll receive. That is why those who oversee or direct employees reach more people with their service and are usually paid handsomely. Those who work entry level jobs with easy tasks are usually paid the minimum wage because the majority of their services require less work. There are of course, exceptions and should not be taken as a matter of fact.

What should you make of your time? If you go from potential employer to other possible employers asking for a job or a finite service, it will prove to be difficult. Most people go out there gung-ho and run to every single place with a resume. While they should be commended for their hard work and effort; they may become discouraged with the lack of interested employers.

Then after turning an application or resume into every feasible employment in a 15 mile radius, they do something contrary to what they started. They quit. They throw in the towel because they're burnt out of energy and motivation. You need to ration your energy and motivation and keep it going strong if you want to make it.

Example of how to spend your time: If you search for a job for one to two hours every day, five days a week, that is five to ten hours a week and twenty to forty hours a month.

	Day 1	Day 2	Day 3	Day 4	Day 5	*End of Week*	*End of Month Total*
1 Hour	1	1	1	1	1	*5*	*20 Hours*
2 Hours	2	2	2	2	2	*10*	*40 Hours*

That is where this book comes in. By broadening your scope of potential income with some of the ideas listed in this book, you can make nearly as much money as you *need* if not more every week for food, bills, paying debts, extra money, or savings. Not to mention that while you're providing these services you get your name out there – more people know of your circumstances – and the more help you now have increasing your potential to finding employment again.

Take for example someone standing on a street corner asking for money. They are waiting for the pity and good-hearted nature of people to throw them a dollar. It's undignified. Yet they do it because they don't understand the fundamental truth: service comes before pay. You cannot start a fire and expect it to be strong at first, then throw the wood in to make it last. You must first do the work, then start the fire, and then you will receive what you were seeking.

Do not be downhearted with early results – most roaring fires likewise start with just a little spark or flame.

There are 101 *starting points* or *ideas* in this book. Improve upon them, simplify them, or use them to help you come up with many more ideas. You can choose to continue to seek employment or solely do what is listed for income. You also have the secret to making money which is **service to others**. There are two more key ingredients that are missing that will guarantee you success.

<u>Set goals</u> and <u>be positive</u>. These two things should be inseparable. You may have a fueled up motivation ready to go out and get to work... but where are you going?

You must set goals for yourself if you want to keep your enthusiasm alive and see the progress you have attained. They point you in the right direction, they *get* work done, help keep organization, and give purpose to your life. Unlike the mentioned beggar on the street corner, it will give you dignity. A goal can be as big as you want or as small as you need it to be so it's more believable to you. This brings me to the second part of this key ingredient for success.

Keep yourself positive. Everyone is appreciative of a cheerful giver – even if it is service that they are giving. It will help you continually receive more work to do and others will enjoy your work as well as your company with them. This state of mind that you can *choose* will help you reach your goals with hardly feeling the bumps on the road. But why should you be positive? Because whatever is out there that you want – it is your right as a human being to have it. YOU deserve to have it and you CAN. Most people think of themselves as expendable. And you may think the same, that you are worthless or nothing special at all.

(All the materials that make up the human body, if you broke it down to an elemental level are relatively cheap and can be bought for little money).

However, the potential you hold is amazing and yet you may not realize it. (For instance a single human body has enough potential atomic energy to keep the United States powered for 16 years!) And just like the atomic energy we all have within us yet unassumingly posses, we have the potential to do extraordinary things even if we may not *feel* like we can at first. You must believe before you can achieve.

We must remember how to learn and adapt instead of trying to fit new possibilities into the mold of our old routines. We all have to fall before we learn to walk, and no one expects you to run. We all just hope you continue to get up. With each attempt you will find yourself going farther each time, growing more as an individual and gaining something that is more valued than a diploma – experience.

HOME CARE

1. Clean Carpets – Rent a carpet cleaner to clean people's carpets, office buildings or even rugs. Gas is not cheap these days so after you have clients, try to make a route and target neighborhoods that have cats or dogs and especially puppies, because they'll need your help. If you schedule it right you can make decent money each week. Tip: Invest in business cards. A good website is **www.vistaprint.com**. They have a good variety of cards, and can help advertise your business even further. We've used this website personally and it's worth it.

2. **Drywall Repair** – Most people will have at least one hole they wouldn't mind having patched up. The materials will last you more than one job and it's a good investment. If you're already doing one house on a street, go next door and show them that you have more drywall materials left, and wouldn't mind working on something for them if they need any repairs. Here's a list of items you will need: **Drywall** or **sheetrock**, a **hammer** and **nails**, **drywall tape**, **drywall compound**, and **saw** or **blade**. Also, let clients know the cost *before* you start working.

3. **Paint** – depending on the climate offer a painting service for homeowners. During the summer, there are many projects that need to be done from the effects of winter. Try looking for houses that need touch-ups on the outside. If they want you to do so then grab yourself a ladder and get started on the opportunity. To speed up the process use a paint sprayer; it saves both you and the homeowner's time. Tip: When you are working always hydrate yourself! You don't want any accidents while on other people's property. Plus it shows that you are responsible. While you're on the outside, ask if they need anything done inside. If they do get a roller instead of a brush, to speed up the process, but do use a paint brush for the edges, corners and for fine touches.

4. **Rent a Room** – Take that unused space above your garage or your basement and turn it into a room for rent. College students and young couples are always looking for a nice place to stay. This would be an excellent opportunity if you live close to a college. Some needs should be met before you put an ad in the newspaper. First, clear out all personal belongings. Second, make sure you have plumbing available for a bathroom and kitchen. Third, remodeling if you need to and tidying up to make things look new and welcoming. Try to design the apartment with the amount of space you have.

Also rent money every month should be equivalent on the size of the space. It's going to help you pay off your house mortgage and maybe profit. If you don't feel comfortable about opening your home to a stranger, then do a background check so you don't miss out on this opportunity – especially if your house can handle it.

5. **Clean Gutters** – Offering to clean gutters won't always land you the job. But if you convince them with the facts, you might be surprised how homeowner's wouldn't mind paying you at least $20 for an hour's work. For instance, facts like preventing damage to their house, the spouting system and their yard from flooding will change their mind. Wear gloves and have a bucket to scoop out the dead leaves. Keep trash bags with you to dispose of the leaves or mess.

6. **Wash Windows** – Not many people like to do this, so that's where you come in. Things you basically need are common window cleaning supplies, like water and ammonia, and paper towels or a squeegee. You can target businesses and homes. It'll only take a short while to complete and it benefits both parties. Also prepare for windows that are too high by having a ladder with you.

7. **Musical Instrument Repair** – If you have knowledge of musical instruments, this can be a genuine money making niche. You can retune or repair damaged instruments at people's homes. Another source of income is buying broken instruments, fixing them, and then selling it for a higher value. Advertise your service in a local newspaper or by internet, signs, or word of mouth.

8. **Trim Tree Branches** - This will prevent damages to vehicles and homes. Even the removal of dead limbs will improve the look of the tree. You'll need a ladder and a pole saw to get branches that are out of reach. If it's a small job use hedge clippers; this will help get the look you're trying to accomplish.

9. **Plant Flowers** – Seeds are relatively cheap and are sold almost everywhere. A lot of people enjoy beautiful flowers but just don't know how to plant them or keep them alive. You have an easy job by sharing your ideas of what type of flowers and arrangements that would look wonderful with their style of home. Sometimes the gardener forgets or didn't have time to water the flowers. You might be able to make some reoccurring income by offering to take care of the flowers every day out of the week. How nice would that be for the home owner to know it's taken care of.

10. **Rake Leaves** – This isn't a chore most people like to do. It seems to me like the leaves always fall right after I'm done raking the yard. To prevent this from occurring, a nice tip is to shake the tree branches so they don't keep falling while you are raking. It is hard work, but for someone who needs money for food, it can provide a meal for the family or food for at least a week. Really all you need is a rake and trash bags. However, if you have an electric powered leaf blower that is a good way to speed up the process (Note the reason I say electrically powered is because of the rising cost of gasoline).

11. **Mow Yards** – Target people or older folks who are just too busy and don't want to pay $70 or more for someone "professional" to mow their yards. Take a push mower if you have one because, they'll be the cheapest on gas. Tip: charge $15 per acre if the person has 3 acres that would be $45 for about an hour and a half of work.

12. **Weed Removal** – Buy a bottle of weed killer at the local store. Travel up and down the streets of your neighborhood offering a weeding service. All you have to do is go to the back yard and front yard and spray. If you want a reoccurring job or recommendation, make sure you're thorough about killing all the weeds so people will hire you again. Not everyone wants chemicals sprayed on their yard, so by pulling the weeds growing in driveways and sidewalks should be removed by hand. This can be a hard and miserable job if you don't wear gloves to protect your hands, and it's nice to have a mat for your knees. Wear a hat so you stay a little cooler and won't get sunburned. Make sure you have all of the necessary tools with you to get the roots, and have a trash bag with you to dispose of all the weeds. Also, make sure to have something to drink to avoid dehydration from being outside all day.

13. **Trim Hedges** – This is something a lot of people neglect and a nice trim can make a home look more inviting and well-kept. It's not that much work and easy to do. Tip: use a tarp to catch the debris – it will make your job so much easier. You can charge by the size of the job so it's reasonable for the homeowners. People will appreciate the little touch ups.

14. **Curb Side Address** – get some number stencils and you can make a good amount of money, offering to spray paint homeowner's addresses on the curb. This helps identify the house, which is good in case of an emergency or to help the pizza guy. It'll help him to not drive around for an extra 15 minutes and making the pizza cold. If you're going to make someone a really nice curbside address, make sure to have a binder of fonts that you like to use, so they can pick. Tip: go to **www.1001freefonts.com**. They have more than 1001 fonts for you to

"Custom Preview". By clicking on "Custom Preview" you can show people all the numbers by typing in "1234567890." Now you have all the numbers to make any combination for any house. Use the website to your advantage for any special requests. Once you get their request, go to a store that has posters. Use the posters to make stencils of the numbers. This part requires art skills, so find an artistic friend to help you or if you can do it yourself.

15. **Sweep Driveways** – First, clear off the home owner's driveway. Second, make sure to have a large push broom so you can get done in no time. Also have a little broom for touch ups. This can make the homes appearance a lot more presentable and clean.

16. **Power Washing** –You can power wash the sidings of homes, trailers, and buildings to give it a fresh look. You can also power wash their driveway which actually cleans the concrete. If you do not own a power washer, schedule jobs throughout the day and rent one. This can be a small investment in how much you earn back. Another business deal can be with fast food restaurants. They will hire people to come and power wash the parking lot to give their business a cleaner look.

17. **Shovel Driveways or Walkways** – Who lives in the northern part of the world and doesn't get this? You can get some cold hard cash for your efforts. Not to mention it's a breeze if you already own a snow thrower.

18. **Salt Driveway or Walkways** – You won't always have shovel snow, but you can remove ice. The elderly population will be very grateful for the removal of one of their worst fears. You don't have to use anything but salt. However, use a spade shovel to chip away at the ice to save on rock salt. Also you can knock off the icicles on the gutters so it doesn't damage the spouting system. Whether you're chipping off the ice or knocking off icicles, remove the pieces of ice out of the way for the homeowners so they don't injure themselves.

19. **Clean Foreclosed Homes** – Banks and retail agencies will actually pay you to clean up, fix up, and sometimes completely redo a foreclosed home so they can resell it for what it's worth or more. This will require a lot of hard work so this will be for people who have experiences in cleaning and other qualifications.

20. **House Sit** – Some home owners will want you to stay at their house when they are gone to prevent being a target of robbery. If that's the case then first, realize this job is based on trust so don't do anything that can break that trust. Second, get their phone numbers or any contact information in case of an emergency. Third, remember to take out their trash and get the mail. Fourth, make sure the house is clean when they come back. Leave a nice thank you note for being trusted to watch their home while they were gone.

21. **Take Out Trash** – It's something just about everyone hates to do or forgets to do. Charge people a dollar every time you take the trash out to the curb. Most people put little value on a dollar and are willing to spend it to get rid of an inconvenience. If you have about 100 people to do this service for, you'll get paid a dollar each house. Say it takes you about two hours to do those 100 homes – you could be making close to $50 an hour every week. That's not bad!

22. **House Keeping** – Keep homes nice and tidy for others who are far too busy. You can charge weekly to just come in and keep up with the sweeping and dusting. That makes all the difference sometimes. If you have cleaning experience, this would be a great way to get back in the field. Even though you're cleaning, dress appropriately and do not show up in men's basketball shorts and a big T-shirt. Appearance is the first impression; if you keep yourself clean then they know you'll do a good job in keeping their home clean.

MIND YOUR OWN BUSINESS

23. Freelance Graphic Design – Are you good with making things eye catching? Offer to help various companies with advertising. You don't always have to create. You can help companies make adjustments and improve advertisements that already exist. This will be easier for you, and if it brings them more attention, they will ask more often for your opinion. This can lead into a more stable and permanent job or you can work with a multitude of different companies on the side.

24. Sell Logos –Some companies are in dire need of a logo makeover. I cannot stress this enough. Some of the logos they have are an eye sore. You can always pitch new ideas that can earn you a big profit. (Nike bought their logo for about $35 – think of how much that person could have really made!) Small businesses will be a target you will want to look at to help. They will be more flexible and more open minded.

25. Make or Design Invitations – This can be for weddings, graduations, or just parties in general. This, believe it or not, can really turn into something big. If you have a creative side and like stationary and scrapbooking materials, you can make interesting invitations for people. Go to a card stock store for the materials you need. Make some practice cards till they are perfect and then make as many as you want. The least amount of invitations you should make is 10. If you want to do more, make it wedding related. Sell your ideas! They are worth more than you know!

26. Translator – Translate things from English to Spanish, or vice versa for any language. This is directed more for people who live in a bi-lingual area having frequent visitors from out of town. If you have a tour guide institution in your area, your ability can be invaluable.

27. Transcribing Service – Have people say whatever they want on a voice recorder that they might want to have written down. Then your job is to listen to the recording and type it for them. Obliviously, this would pay better if someone has a longer recording. I've had this done for me with another book, saving me a lot of time and energy. Charge by minute or by the overall job.

28. Dance Lessons – Not everyone can dance, but you can show them how. This can turn into a class of students. You can do what you love and make money at the same time! With all the different types of dance out there, possibilities are nearly endless in what you'll specialize in. Brush up on the history of the dance you choose to teach so you can educate your students. It comes off very professional and makes it more interesting. Make sure to keep your class fun and clean. Most importantly make sure you have plenty of room and no valuables around the area to prevent damages. You can either, charge each student in a dance class, or do private lessons and charge by the hour.

29. In Home Haircuts – Why go to the barbershop or salon when someone who is licensed comes to you to do just about the same thing? It saves people gas and the expensive costs of salons. If you, a stylist, have problems with your current employer, but love what you do then this would be a great idea. If you don't like driving all the time, then have people come to your house but charge cheaper than the salons so they would rather come to you. It's at least a 90% profit for you and you'll be happier.

30. Photography – Baby pictures to Wedding pictures – you can sell your pictures to local newspapers as a freelance photographer. This is a very wide range of what you can do with a camera and who your target consumer can be. Make sure you get some practice pictures before you advertise yourself so you can show your customers what you can do.

31. Art Lessons – Art is something people want to do. Art is another method for someone to express themselves. Specialize in making paintings, realistic art, sculptures, or cartoons. Although it's an artist's habit to undermine their talent, don't if you know what you're doing and wouldn't mind teaching others. It's an amazing feeling for people who aren't as talented at art to actually create something. You don't have to do anything like Michael Angelo, but something small and fun might just be what some people want to do. And maybe later you can start an advanced class for the more difficult things, but make sure it is something you can teach.

32. Driving Lessons – Driving lessons from the BMV cost so much money these days! This service can help people who lack confidence in their driving or just learning to drive. The goal can be to help your customer pass their driver's test and obtain their driver's license. Even at that there are plenty of people who can still use a few lessons to get better at driving for an example, parallel parking.

33. Grocery Shopper – This would be great for older people who live alone or for the extremely busy people. Some would forget to eat if they didn't have breakfast, lunch and dinner in an ordered list. You can offer to help buy and deliver their groceries at their expense. For example, you can set up payment options with a flat rate fee of $50 per week to provide this service. You can also charge by the quantity of food you bought and the cost of gas. Shop for multiple people and set up a delivery route for your convenience.

34. Become a Handyman – Offer to do little things like: stopping a leak in the faucet, leaking in the roof, or fixing cabinet doors, etc. You can post your availability on places like Craigslist for free to start. Who knows, it may even lead you into actual employment.

35. Become a Consultant – If you're good with money, accounting, or familiar with the laws of the court system, you can charge people to seek out your advice on how they should proceed. You could even help them plan for future things like retirement. Your advice is valuable and there are people who need it.

36. Sell Bottled Water – Go to a local fair or concert and sell cold bottled water to people for a $1 each. That will probably be cheaper than what other places are selling it for, plus not to mention, you probably only spent $5 for a pack of 35 bottles of water. That can be a huge profit in a very short time!

Here's an example, if you buy a pack of 35 bottles of water for $5 and then sell each bottle for $1 that comes to a total of $35. That's a $30 profit off a $5 investment.

37. **Event Planner** – There are a lot of events you can help someone plan for. Such as, weddings, graduations, baby showers, and family reunions! There are unlimited amounts of ideas for planning a party. There are people out there who want a party but cannot handle the stress. Let the party store know about your service. If you help their business – they will help you by recommending your services to people in the future. If you're professional, good at organization, and can live up to expectations, then you can expect referrals.

38. **Courier** – People are willing to pay extra money for packages to be delivered on the same day. How fast and how well you organize your deliveries will increase your speed and efficiency. It may even earn you an extra tip or more customers. Make sure to handle all packages or whatever you transport with great care.

39. **Baby Sit** – Watch the neighborhood kids or expand to being a Nanny. If you love children and know how to care for them, this would be something for you to look into. There are courses online so you can become a certified baby sitter, but many have not taken this course and can still get the job. However, a very important thing to invest in or think about is CPR certification in case of an emergency you could save a child.

40. **Chop Firewood** – Now this is hard work, but a chainsaw can make this overwhelming task not so burdensome. And while you do that you can turn the wood into usable fire wood. This can be for the home owner for an additional fee or haul it away and sell it. You can offer an additional service to remove trees and unwanted bushes for an additional fee. *Some states may require a permit to sell fire wood.

41. **In Home Manicures or Pedicures** – You can really turn your income around if you are really good at doing nails. Set up appointments for clients as a salon would, but visit them at their home for their convenience. This could be advertised as a service that you could never get at a salon! Make sure you have a license. If you don't but you're still really good at doing nails then charge your friends and family. If you have talent they may not care if you work at a salon or have a license. (Note this is for basic manicures). All this money could go towards schooling or paying off bills.

42. Create Jewelry – This can be accomplished with beads or even reused pieces of older jewelry. You can do so much here if you have the time and ideas. You can make earrings, necklaces, bracelets, rings, and even ankle bracelets! Another thing people don't think about making is belly jewelry! Now I don't mean belly button jewelry but jewelry that goes around your hips to accent the hip area. It can be used during the summer time for the beach or just to make a regular outfit a little more fun. If you have pieces of old jewelry, wash it and use it as a focus point of the new necklace or bracelet. Possibilities are endless and the more expensive the beads, the more you can charge. Go to craft stores to find a large assortment of beads.

43. **Sewing Things or Repair** – once upon a time most people had a tailor in their town. The absence of this profession can help you make some extra money, by repairing small tears, rips, or if you are really good, go for full tailoring. People may want to save an extra dollar by getting the item of clothing fixed rather than buying something brand new. This is an easy job to get into. Just let everyone you know you are good with sewing and tailoring. Before you know it you'll have people asking you to fix their dresses, shirts, pants – everything! Altering wedding dresses would be a big profit, but only if you do it right. Keep in mind; wedding dresses are a big deal so make sure you have the "okay" by the bride to do anything to the dress.

44. **Rent a Truck or Van** – Not everyone has a truck or a van to move large furniture, dirt, or even junk. Rent out your vehicle! Just make sure it's insured. You don't want to run into any problems with the Law and lose your business let alone your vehicle. If you don't feel comfortable letting people drive your truck or van then do the driving for them. Hey, while you're at it, help them move and charge extra if you want.

45. **Pet Sit** – Watch someone's pet while their out of town. Take them home with you, but make sure you have everything you'll need for the pet. First, make sure you have food, leash, crate, any medicine, or anything the pet needs on a daily basis, etc. Usually you only need the basics, but every pet owner is different. If you can't have pets at your house or apartment then stay at their house. Go on a regular basis to feed and let the pet outside. Depending on what pet it is, make sure to exercise or play with it, clean the pet's area and if need to take them to their vet appointments.

46. **Tutoring** – Subjects such as Math, Science and English Literature, do not come easy to a great number of people. If you are naturally talented in a subject you can teach it to others. There are many parents who would lovingly spend top dollar for their children to have a better understanding to improve their grades in school. Tutoring can last for more than a few sessions. You can end up helping the student throughout their educational career, maybe even well into college. This can be very rewarding service in many aspects.

47. **Pet Waste Removal** – This might not be the most glamorous job in the world, but you can for sure make this into a profitable business. Make sure to advertise at local dog parks or your veterinarian's office. If you schedule it as a weekly service, you'll always have income and you'll be more organized in getting the work done faster. Also, a good tip is to donate 10 to 30 % of the profits from your work to an organization like the ASPCA to help animals in need. Pet owners will always have a soft spot for animals in need because of the love for their own. This will increase their willingness to hire you to do the job. This benefits you, animals in need, and the home owner.

48. **Home Carwashes** – People are busy so help them out and keep them happy by cleaning their car. Offer specialized services such as waxing, polishing and even a complete detailing for them for an additional fee. Bring the equipment you need, but get the water supply from the home you're working at.

49. **Teach Music Lessons** – There are a lot of people who have and own musical instruments but don't know how to play them – yet alone play them well. Like other jobs listed, offer your service in the newspaper, online, posters, or word of mouth. Set up lessons tailored to your students schedule or even set up classes to teach multiple people on a specific instrument. They are just waiting to be taught!

50. **Dog Walking** – Dogs need to be exercised. Being crammed up inside all day or chained up in the back yard doesn't make a happy pet. Regular exercise can calm the dog's temperament and can help alleviate, if not stop, some unwanted behaviors. Exercise will wear out the dog and will be better behaved for pet owners when they arrive home. Both are ready to relax and eat dinner. Tip: brush up on breed types and inform the owner of the needs of their dogs. You can then tailor your walk or activity to the dog. This specialized care and concern for the pet will make you stand out from the others trying to do the same thing.

51. **Make Signs** – Help others advertise their moving sale, garage sale, or etc. You can make vanity signs for 'him' or 'her,' no swimming signs, or if you're in a high tourist area – make a sign that would be a nice souvenir of their vacation or trip, for people to take home. You can use sheet metal, cardboard, poster board, and wood as basic materials.

52. **Oil Change** – Just another convenience rather than dealing with frustrating appointments and waiting hours at the dealership. You can do it for a fraction of the time and get people's business. It's a dirty job, but not a whole lot of work. Just make sure the car hasn't been driven much before you change the oil to reduce any risk of getting burned. Include a few fees such as proper oil clean up and removal afterword since dumping oil is not only harmful to the environment it is also illegal. Transportation charges can help pay for gas.

53. **Clean Office Buildings** – Many people actually make this their career. Clean several offices a day or during the middle of the night while no one is there. Most offices supply their own cleaning equipment for you to use. The nicer and cleaner it looks, the more you'll have a consistent job. It's a tough economy now, so if some places already have a cleaning crew, you may want to try to negotiate a lower price than your competition to get the job.

54. **Fix Computers** – If you know how to work with computers or repair them, you can be paid generously for your help. It doesn't even have to be fixing computers but you can actually teach. Yes, TEACH people how to use their computer. What do you have to lose for something that may come naturally to you? Be patient when teaching, and come up with easy ways for them to remember or make signs by the computer to serve as memory triggers for your learning customers.

55. **Can Food** – Food doesn't last forever but if you have the equipment or knowledge, canning food for others helps extend the quality and the life of home grown food. This can save your customer a lot of money by saving food in the long run. There are many cook books you can use for canning ideas. This is great for making Jam or Jelly that you could sell too!

56. **Personal Trainer** – Many people have a gym set at home but don't really know how to use it to its potential. Others join a local gym but do not get the full benefit from it. Here's where you come along and show them how to get in shape, be healthy, and stick to their diet. Also you'll be a consistent motivation and a partner to work out with. Always be patient and understand your client's limitations.

57. **Designated Transportation** – Contact a local bar to provide a safe drive home for the people who have drank too much. This service will be beneficial for everyone. It keeps drunk drivers off the road and prevents harming other people's safety. So you're keeping people safe and not to mention it puts money in your pocket.

58. **Pet Training** – This can be from potty training to fetch and even to stay off the couch. Pet training can be a good field to get into if you love animals. This isn't limited to dogs or cats. Birds and other animals can learn some neat tricks too if you know the proper way to teach them. Get into contact with local pet stores like PetSmart, depending on where you live they might have the program for pet training. Regardless make sure to treat the pet with care and patience. Also you can show the pet owner tips and suggestions when they are training with their pet at home.

59. **Teach another Language** – Teaching people another language requires patience and organization skills. In this ever diverse world, you will find this skill to be more needed as time goes on. You can teach Spanish, French, German, Chinese, or whatever language you know well. You can set up your own classes or private lessons to teach people the basics, reading, and writing. Make sure to set up lesson plans and give out homework for your student to work on. Keep in mind this could even be English. Sometimes when people talk about teaching another language, we tend to forget the ones who need help with their English. So, don't sell yourself short from this idea if you know English and don't mind teaching others!

60. **Become a Tour Guide** – If you live in a popular city or an area around celebrities, giving tourists a guide would be a fun job especially, if you know the city like the back of your hand. It will be like a walk in the park (Figuratively and perhaps literally). People who take tours usually love being educated on where they are and what significant event happened there. So make sure you know your history of where you are taking people. Also, scheduling a route will save people time in their day. You can have a container or something more interesting available for tips to make extra money.

61. **Gift Wrapping** – This would be lucrative around holidays. Not everyone has that special skill of wrapping presents neatly. I know I wouldn't mind paying someone a few dollars to wrap up my gift beautifully. You may have noticed corporate companies in the mall are doing it already. They charge $3-$7 for wrapping gifts during the holidays or for just any special occasion. You can do the same thing at your own home, for less if not the nice price. All you have to do is buy nice, all event-related wrapping paper and get some pretty bows of all different sizes – and advertise!

62. **Do Taxes for Others** – I hate doing my taxes, and I'm sure about 97% of the population does too. If this is something that doesn't bother you much and you know how to do very well there are plenty of people who need your help. So ask friends, neighbors or relatives if you can prepare their tax return. Most likely they will take your offer and pay you ahead of time or pay you by their tax return. You can post ads in the newspaper, just make sure you advertise your qualifications as well as your service. I recommend taking tax prepare course – you may be liable if you make mistakes.

63. **Iron Clothes** – It might sound crazy, but there are some people who don't know how to properly iron clothes. You can help by ironing their clothes and advertise a same day delivery service. Keep track of what you have ironed throughout the day. Then make a route for what needs to be delivered, this will truly be helpful and profitable to you. Most dry cleaners cannot come close to that service. Always think outside the box to make a profit.

64. **Ticket Broker** – Make extra money by buying tickets for a cheaper price at the beginning of the sports season, or when concert tickets go on sale. Ticketmaster.com has tickets, event dates and specials you can check on from time to time. Sell the tickets when you think they are worth the most value leading up to the event. You can even put the tickets for sale on Craigslist or eBay.

65. **Window Tinting** – The products to tint car windows or any windows are sold in most auto part stores. This can earn you some money if you get good at what you do. This is good for extra privacy in cars as well in homes. There are many different types of film out there to tailor to your individual customer.

66. **Make Gardens** – Make gardens for people and for a weekly fee, take care of it. Plant food of whatever they want to grow. This could be from berries to watermelons.

This will help the homeowner eat better and in the long run save on groceries. Don't tell your children but you can actually make some good money playing in dirt all day!

67. Sell Fruits and Vegetables – People don't have to buy fruit or vegetables at the store. Sell whatever you may grow in your own garden for some extra cash. Besides, most people prefer home grown food over chemically treated fruit and vegetables any day. The more variety you offer the more customers you'll get.

68. Car Pooling – This is a good idea if you have a big vehicle like a van. Talk to fellow employees who may live around your area and offer them this service. Charge by person and take them to and from work. The individual saves money on gas, because it's cheaper to have you drive every week than to put in $50 or more for gas. If you're a parent of a student talk to other parents to provide a similar service to pick up and drop off their children. I know some parents are going to prefer this, than to have their child walk or ride the bus. If you decide to make this a small business on the side you may be able to claim the gas money you spent as a write off for your taxes. Tip: keep all your receipts!

Things to Sell

69. **Pawn unused or old items** – This can definitely help you get some extra money. Not to mention if you have a good eye, buy stuff at a garage sale and pawn it for more money than you bought it for.

70. **Hold a Bake Sale** – Who doesn't love baked goods? Set up your own stand at a festival or even collaborate with others to make an even bigger event. This will definitely help raise money. Also contact locally owned grocery stores and see if you can set up a small stand in the store.

71. **Sell Sandwiches for Office Buildings** – Granted this may depend on where you live if you are allowed to loiter or sell on public grounds. But one thing is for sure – instead of leaving work, going through traffic, dealing with everyone else on their lunch break, and then rushing back to work to eat super fast, people would rather just come outside, where you'll be standing and pay for a homemade sandwich. This practical idea can be used with other items to sell.

72. **Sell T-Shirts** – You can make your own designs or sell them for people. There are websites online you can make your own stuff for free. Either way this can be a nice trick at earning money. I have a store at www.Zazzle.com/thetqast that I made over a year ago that provides a passive income without me working for it at all. It's not hard to set up and they do most if not all the work for you. Other sites like Zazzle.com are:

Cafepress.com
CustomInk.com
UberPrints.com
SpreadShirt.com

73. **Recycle** – Aluminum cans, bottles, metal, and other recyclables can be sold to recycling centers for money. Not to mention you're helping the environment. You can also have people who want to help the environment pay you to take and recycle things for them. So you get paid for recycling and helping people with their recyclables. I know this may sound gross, but for some extra cash go to parks and see what the trash looks like. If you see anything you can get money for, go for it!

74. Submit Articles to Newspapers – Use your skill as a writer or story teller to get an article in the newspaper. Make sure to have your portfolio so you can present your writing style. This can be done online to various news websites as well. Eventually who knows where that may lead you?

75. Sell Your Hair / Bodily Fluids – If this doesn't bother you or your conscience – there are facilities that will buy – well, you. Selling semen isn't too uncommon anymore and there are some places that will pay a couple thousand at least, to women who sell their eggs. Now I'm not talking about selling your hair to be made into a wig. Rather I'm talking about actual hair transplants where they remove the hair at the follicle and will place it into another person to grow as their own hair.

76. Sell Gold or Silver – These are always going to be worth something. If you have some extra gold or silver lying around, it may be worth selling, or to provide for your family. The price for gold for example can change over time. Right now gold is at an all time high and you'll get more money for your trade for it.

77. **Sell your Books** – Yes it is actually possible to sell older books you may own. MyBookBank.com is just one way of getting rid of unread or used books for extra spending money.

78. **Garage Sale** – Well this is kind of obvious right? But everyone loves garage sales. I know my wife goes crazy for them. Put up some signs letting people who are passing by know where to head. It's about 98% profit in cash.

79. **Make Pottery** – Plates, cups and vases to name a few. Use some paint supplies to color your work to make them more eye catching. Even offer to custom work and charge a little bit extra. Be sure to do your homework on the many different types of clay that will help you get the different results in the quality and look of your finished pottery.

80. **Knit** – Sweaters, blankets, quilts, hats, baby blankets/sweater/hats, and mittens. This would be more for the winter time but you can quilt blankets during the summer to prepare for winter's profits. Again, doing personal requests can earn you extra money.

81. **Make Bird Houses** –You can make your own bird house. Use what Mother Nature gives you for free. There are many different types of bird houses you can make. For example there's traditional, modern, or a mixture of both, etc. Or you can buy the ones already made at the craft store and decorate them the way you like. Try to create more unique designs. The possibilities are endless. Invest in your creations by renting booths at festivals or fairs.

82. **Animal Feeders** –This has the same concept as bird houses. Create your own animal feeder and then sell them. Animal feeders can be for any type of animal. Animals like squirrels, chipmunks, deer, etc. can be enjoyable to watch. This can be entertaining to watch in your own home. Be creative and express yourself freely.

83. **Sell paintings** – People love art. Help them fill their empty walls. Rent a booth at festivals or fairs and sell your paintings. Make an investment for a profit. You are always able to put up an interactive gallery online and sell you work over the internet too.

Easy Money

84. **Focus Groups** – This job pays you for your opinions, views, attitudes or beliefs toward a product, or to be part of a survey. This is usually used to increase the effectiveness of marketing to the consumer or help companies identify who their target consumer is. Find opportunities in your local employment guide or the employment classified section of your local newspaper. You can also find opportunities online on popular job searches.

85. **Mystery Shopper** – This is where you buy everyday things that you would normally. However, you take a survey to evaluate what you bought or how the service was in the store. For example:

- the types of products shown
- the sales arguments used by the employee
- how the employee attempted to close the sale
- whether the employee suggested any add-on sales
- whether the employee invited the shopper to come back to the store
- cleanliness of store and store associates
- speed of service
- how long it takes before the mystery shopper is greeted
- whether or not the greeting is friendly

Companies employ mystery shoppers to improve the overall customer experience and increase the effectiveness of their marketing. Legitimate companies do not charge an application fee. Many accept applications online. If this interests you start your search at www.mysteryshop.org .

86. **Human Test Subject** – Drug companies who get the "okay" for testing products on humans pay rather well. Although you may want to research before you volunteer your body to science, especially if you have a history of medical complications or allergies. Look for these opportunities online on popular job searches.

87. **Elderly Companion** – Take them to the doctors, watch TV with them, or just be there for to talk. If you go through an agency they will do a thorough background check and a drug test before they match you with anyone. Look for local agencies in your area that can aid you in this aspect. Different agencies can be located by looking in the phone book, local job search or online.

88. **Human Billboard** – You will see people standing on the side of the road begging for money or maybe you have done that yourself. Well why not get paid to do the same thing, but instead attract traffic to promote stores. For example, tax season is a popular time when tax offices will pay people to draw attention to their business.

89. **Phone Book Delivery**– This may be a tough job – but get into contact with Yellowpages or another local phone company and get paid to deliver phone books where they specify. Some companies will pay by the job or by the hour. Be sure you can physically handle this task before you try to attempt because it can be strenuous on your body.

90. **Newspaper Delivery** – This isn't a hard gig to get and it will only really require most of the time in your mornings. This used to be done by bicycle so if you don't have a car it's not a big deal, you can still make this work. Although for the winter time, you might want to use other means of transportation to keep warm and make things easier. The more routes you take on, the more money you earn.

91. **Advertise on your Car** – Companies will gladly pay you to advertise using your car. It's simple – you just get the sticker or magnet and drive around! Make sure to do your research and be certain the company will pay you for using your car. Some companies will look at your driving records before hiring you after all you are representing them while you drive.

92. **Become Famous** – If you keep your eyes peeled you'll see ads for actors/actresses; stand-ins or just extras needed in a TV show, movie or commercial. Also keep your ears open because they advertise such opportunities on the radio. It's not a reoccurring job but you can be paid a couple hundred dollars for a couple days of work.

Opportunities Online

93. **Play World of Warcraft** – What? Yes I'm serious. People use a character to get them up to a high level and sell them online. You can actually make a lot of money and you're playing a video game all day! This is a great idea for kids to help pay the bills – might as well do something with all the video games they play all day every day. Search various website forums and look for potential buyers.

94. **Online Surveys** – This I recommend if you're just bored, enjoy taking surveys, and want some extra cash. There are a variety of company websites that pay you to take online surveys. It's an easy job but it takes patience and a lot of time.

95. **Sell on eBay or Craigslist** – It's like a never ending garage sale. You can sell whatever you want when you want, without setting up tables, signs, and sitting outside all day. On eBay or craigslist it's priced a little higher and will take a little longer but you can do other money making ideas while waiting. Ask friends and family if there's anything they want to sell. If they are interested then make a deal on a percentage of the profit. So that way they make money and you will too. There are actually eBay stores that do this for people so you can to!

96. **Make Websites** – You can make personal or businesses website for people. Sometimes offering to redo someone's website can get you the job. Websites are hard for some people to comprehend and making one would be ridiculously hard to do. If you have knowledge about technology and that natural talent with computers, go for it. Tip: For additional income, charge a monthly maintenance fee. All you have to do is make sure everything is still in working order and keep up with updates.

97. **Start a Blog** – If you have an opinion that people like to listen to or read about, make an online blog. The more followers you get the more reputable you become. With your growing popularity you can get paid for just having advertisements on your page. Some advertisements will even pay you for every click it receives from your site. Also blog about a certain products you want to promote if you're an affiliate to that product. There are many other ways to get paid for your blog that aren't mentioned here but this will put you in the right direction.

98. **Affiliate Marketing** – Now advertising someone else's product online for 30% to 50% commission can make you some serious, and I mean serious money. It might start off slow at first, but if you make a practice out of it and know the internet pretty well, this could lead into your retirement. Some people have made millions of dollars by doing this. But this isn't for everyone; it can be very difficult at first. ClickBank.com is a great and easy place to start off. You advertise various products for others and if people go through your link and buy the product, you earn commission from the sale. Be cautious of ones who want to teach you the so called tricks and secrets to making it big but charge you hundreds of dollars to learn.

99. **How-to videos on YouTube** – Again you can provide a service of teaching others something you may know how to do very well and still make money. Have it linked to an eBay page where you sell a specific item, or put advertisements on your video. There are hundreds of ways to make money doing something in this way.

Misc.

100. **Write a Book** – Fill what you know in a book to teach others, or if you're a good story teller create a story. If you have interesting views that could catch the attention of others, this would be a good topic for you to write about. What if you don't have any views or an imagination to write about? Then write about a very interesting life experience. Even if you don't get it published and put into major book stores, you can always sell and market your books online as an ebook.

101. **Invent** – If you think about it, most inventions are only drastic if not just slight improvements to the things we already have in our lives. There are a thousand types of tires out there, but they are all still the same thing. A wheel. Think how to make something better or more efficient. If you have a radical idea that may even change the world, this is something you should definitely pursue. Always pursue inspired thought because it is a gift. Don't give up! Make sure to protect your idea with a patent. Consider it an investment in yourself. Just remember that the intent needs to be an improvement, a convenience, or something that provides a service to others.